D R E D G I N G

Eileen

Tabios

FOR ATLANTIS

Otoliths

DREDGING FOR ATLANTIS by Eileen Tabios

Design & typesetting
by Mark Young

Front cover image & cover design
by harry k stammer

ISBN-10 0-9775604-4-9
ISBN-13 978-0-9775604-4-8

Printed in USA

Otoliths
8 Kennedy St
Rockhampton
QLD 4700
Australia

WWW: http://the-otolith.blogspot.com

"…if Solon had only, like other poets, made poetry the business of his life, and had completed the tale which he brought with him from Egypt, and had not been compelled, by reason of the factions and troubles which he found stirring in his own country when he came home, to attend to other matters, in my opinion he would have been as famous as Homer or Hesiod, or any poet."

—from Plato's "Timaeus and Critias", translated into English by Benjamin Jowett

Table of Contents

I. DREDGING FOR ATLANTIS

II. Excerpts From "SOMEWHAT OF A CHILDHOOD"

III.   ATHENA'S DIPTYCH

I. DREDGING FOR ATLANTIS

SCUMBLE-D

I cannot remember the name of that seacoast city,
but it trembled

.............................it is near XYZ
a town with hyphens

Now, so many deaths

...........................the only art left—
the preparation of grace

WINGED VICTORY

Defile
that Carrara

A nude woman stands for the universe

All of her names end
with "A"

Then her eyes…

BURNING PULPIT

Could our two miseries
copulate
into one opulent being?

Men simplify
then slink back
to antediluvian burrows

Baby priests
turn away
to cast profiles forsworn to Donatello

But she is clutching lilac print
within a shadow burning
away
salvation's seedlings

GLOW WORM

Out of the severing
a starlight

"Let Joy go solace-winged"

It is whispered:
Rose petals procreate
within the belly of the sun

FUNNY BRASS

Dawn
(like my puppy)
penetrates eyelash drapes

Man becomes
woman
by losing aloofness

"Monotone" transforms to "moonstone"

Go forth and prettily miscalculate

PARENTHETICAL

Coax
lullabyes

from tin cans
long emptied, rusting

A CRYSTALLIZATION

The white street
an obscenity

when haloed ascetics
can't remember
awash in hot water

There must be another light

than this wind stuffing
headless birds
—and spermatozoa—
into fragile craters
of a trapped moon

until even onions
cease to make you cry

LEWD

1)
Sobs
from his abandoned harem

bring down comets
accuse the alcove
smother the zodiac with pink chenille

pomades complaisance
by dictators

2)
Defying idols a past epoch

Schools now mixed in antiquity

3)
Lions bred for locked jaws

4)
All sound flabbergasted

CONSEQUENCE

A breakfast of rain

…………………….oil-silk umbrella

"Count stars for me"

EASILY MEMORIZED

Kept her kindly
amidst his pots and pans
where, wisely, she busied herself

Warm light in the parlor

A crinoline

"Ding Dong" said the bell

Saccharine for his cup

Ever-clean chopping board

"When she was lazy
she wrote a poem
on the milk bill"

P.S.
The first line: "Good morning"

MINOR RIDDLE

Colour of coppered mustard
evokes
the toes of Giovanni Bapini
whose name reigned at a trattoria
opposite the Pitti Palace

Abominable manners
e.g., he would murder a woman
and not attend her funeral

Oh, incandescent breath of civilization!

Minarets growing within muddy whirlpools

Some believe Florence to be a lady
with flowers in her hair

Florence is a city
(interrupting blue sky)
with streets of stones

SHADE

Men pass
their hats not ours

Ourselves
trapped in mirrors

Throbbing
possible only behind curtains

Some virgins
forget how children scratch

"REINFORCING THE HITHERTO NEGLIGIBLE"

Whose essence
......................winks

in the to-and-fro
......................of your cufflinks?

(An occasional snap stings someone's face)

IN PASSING

They see the dolls

For a moment, their eyes relax

CAFÉ DU NEANT

Kohl
tell tales without words

Pricked finger?
Flame of taper?
No matter of consequence

Brandy cherries
wink
as they decompose
in sealed jars

"cabs outside the door"

YOUR

indisputably male voice
roared through my veins

and brain,
you pugilist of intellect

Where is my coffin—
its succoring bed?

CAESURA

A wheel
...........in a rut
jerks back my girl

hedges, then
.................sky

"down covers her thighs"

MARCH

Grey men
falling
……../ fading
to "greyness of stone"

even as the angle of the sun
"cuts the whole lot in half"

In the distance, a noonday cannon
                                            / *canon*

scatters pigeons

A HOBBY

of collecting death-beds

Dear Blue Nun,
.....Wrap the body in flannel
of Anglo-American quality
while round the hotel
wanton Italian matrons
lust for head-waiters

IMPRESSION

of small animal
.....................carcass
covered with blue bottles

"—Epicurean—"

ARS POETICA

I am climbing a distorted mountain

....the summit

s
u
b
s
i
d
e
s into anticipation of
....*Repose*

"which never comes"

FUTURISM

The truants of heaven
possess a startling velocity

BOWERY

........Is ....this.......a
bomb......or......cloud......or
...footnote.....or .....pornography
or......hiccup......or......sugar
...or "the ruined body of poor people"
........or.......Eileen R. Tabios.....or
undeserved fanfare.......or....apple
delivered to Eve......or.....painting
on diaper......or.....the nature of
slyness.......or .....ecstasy....or
.......vermilion

....vermilion

........................vermilion

vermilion
◉ermilion
VERMILION
VERMILION
VERMILION
V!E!R!M!I!L!I!O!N!

THE BIRTH OF A RAINBOW

Innocent excrements
humming their dotage

seduce doves
Occasionally, a cobalt egg

WHITE AS GRECIAN MARBLE

A trolley loaded
with ivory busts

glides against air
overtaken by snow

beyond this crocheted lace
of white dandelions

and one orchid
recalling its youthful orgies

VESUVIAN

Coal among the olives
Olive among the coals

The abbess gambles
to roof her refugees

As the Adriatic sighs and sighs

IMPISH MUSIC

Adolescent eros
a consistent source
for radium
of the Word

! !

Pointillist experiments
pupil mischievous angels

singing
! The Sublime Always Wink !

RELIGION (POE MEETS BRANCUSI)

When nightingales reign
over all clowns

scythes shall melt before mystics

as God reveals himself
thin-ankled but
a peasant

BENIGN SYPHILIS

A city lies
in her belly

There, ashbins
emanate songs

Palm trees refuse hunching
before twilight

Knick-knacks
retain vivacity

Everyone cheerfully picks
lemons in Los Angeles

HAIL TO YOU

Bone of your arm—
.........................such dignity

erasing
these wasted years

NOTES ON *DREDGING FOR ATLANTIS*:

These are ekphrastic poems utilizing the painterly technique of scumbling. From *Merriam-Webster Dictionary*:

>   **scumble**   \ *SKUM-bul* \   *verb*
>
>   *1 a : to make (as color or a painting) less brilliant by covering with a thin coat of opaque or semiopaque color b : to apply (a color) in this manner*
>
>   **2 : to soften the lines or colors of (a drawing) by rubbing lightly*
>
>   *The history of "scumble" is blurry, but the word is thought to be related to the verb "scum," an obsolete form of "skim" (meaning "to pass lightly over"). Scumbling, as first perfected by artists such as Titian, involves passing dry, opaque coats of oil paint over a tinted background to create subtle tones and shadows. But although the painting technique dates to the 16th century, use of the word "scumble" is only known to have begun in the late 18th century. The more generalized "smudge" or "smear" sense appeared even later, in the mid-1800s.*

All of the poems, except for "Scumble-d" textually scumble poems by Mina Loy taken from *The Lost Lunar Baedeker: Poems by Mina Loy*, Selected and Edited by Roger L. Conover (Farrar, Straus, Giroux, New York, 1996). "Scumble-d" sources its underlying inspiration as Derek Walcott's *THE BOUNTY* (The Noonday Press / Farrar, Straus and Giroux, New York, 1997).

The poems (or earlier versions) were first published in: *LuzMag* (Ed. Lars Palm), *MiPOesias* (Ed. Didi Menendez), *Eratio Postmodern Poetry* (Ed. Gregory Vincent St. Thomasino), *Shampoo* (Ed.Del Ray Cross), *melancholia's tremulous dreadlocks* (Ed. Andrew Lundwall) & *Otoliths* (Ed. Mark Young).

"Scumble-d" was presented as a broadside for part of the Inverse Poetry Reading Series, curated by Scott Glassman, in Philadelphia (September 2006) and translated into visual art by Sandra Simonds through*Wildlife Poetry Magazine*.

II.   Excerpts From
"SOMEWHAT OF A CHILDHOOD"

The Bread of Florence

— for Barry Schwabsky

We caught exciting
smells for
an

instant as we
passed—fresh
bread

from a *panetteria*,
the vinegary
tang

of a wineshop,
roasting coffee
from

a grocer's, new
leather from
a

saddler's—as well,
the frequent
whiff

of drains. When
a baker's boy
rings

a doorbell at
that tall
building,

shutters would fling
themselves open
from

above, and ebony-,
long-haired, violet-eyed,
vanilla-scented,

raspberry-lipped, deep-dimpled, low-bloused
Marta would
lean

over the windowsill
cooing, "*Chi
e?*"

Then to save
a long
climb,

a basket on
a chord
would

fall, the bread
placed in
it,

and be hauled
up, hand
over

hand. Bread and
always a
letter —

his always-hungry proxy.

Mont Blanc

Cook sweet chestnuts
then pass
them

through a sieve
woven from
hair.

Mix with chocolate
and brandy
then

cover with whipped
white of
egg

and sugar. But
I do
not

recommend this recipe
for buffet
dinners.

One short-sighted young
man, who
had

taken off spectacles
to impress
a

girl, offered to
serve the
target

of his affections.
He reached
across

to remove what
he thought
was

a china cover —
his hand
disappeared

into the cream.

WIND FALLS

The olives' oil
contents grow
substantially

from October to
December. It's
risky,

however, to leave
them too
long

on trees because
if they
become

"windfalls" they cannot
be considered
for

virgin pressings.

THE MUSHROOM CHAPTER

We watched Fiore
slice mushrooms
delicately

then spread the
thin segments
on

a table or
wood planks
to

dry under the
sun. Afterwards
they

would be hung
in muslin
or

calico bags near
the kitchen
fireplace.

Back in London
each autumn
I

would receive a
bag of
dried

mushrooms. The last
one arrived
in

the autumn of
1939, shortly
after

the outbreak of war.

III. ATHENA'S DIPTYCH

ATHENA BEGINS

My love. If
words can
reach

whatever world you
suffer in—
Listen:

I have things
to tell
you.

At this muffled
end to
another

year, I prowl
somber streets
holding

you—in my
head, this
violence!—

a violent gaze.
You. With
dusk

arrives rain drifting
aslant like
premature

memory. Am I
the one
who

suddenly cleared these
streets? *My*
Love,

all our hours
are curfew
hours—

what I offer
is this
dying

fish into whose
gullet I
have

thrust my thumb.
Why did
you

lose all Alleluias?
My love—
Listen:

ATHENA

What's deemed necessary
changes. Hear
me

listening in another
decade, editing
last

and first lines.
A different
Singer

croons from behind
an impassive
speaker.

I listen, cross
out more
lines.

The poem cannot
be pure.
Sound

never travels unimpeded
by anonymous
butterflies.

Writing it down
merely freezes
flight—

Translation: an inevitable
fall. Take
control

by shooting it
as if
pigeons

were clay: This
one is.
But

it provided pleasure
once, was
"necessary."

Once, it flew
with non-imaginary
wings.

O, clay pigeon.
Translation: the
error

is my ear's.
The sky
ruptured

suddenly—I saw
but did
not

hear the precursor
fall of
leaves.

*****

Edit it down.
Edit it
down.

Silence is Queen,
not lady
-in-waiting.

Edit it down.
Edit it.
Edit

it down. Edit
it. Edit.
Edit.

NOTES ON SECTIONS II & III:

Section II's poems scumble from Kinta Beevor's memoir, *A Tuscan Childhood* (Pantheon Books, New York, 1993).

"The Bread of Florence" was first published in *Dragonfire* (Ed. Henry Israeli).

Section III's poems scumble from John Banville's novel, *Athena* (Vintage Books, New York, 1995).

The poems in Sections II and III are also written in the hay(na)ku form, specifically the reverse hay(na)ku sequence. More information on the hay(na)ku is available at

http://www.baymoon.com/~ariadne/form/haynaku.htm

http://haynakupoetry.blogspot.com

http://www.meritagepress.com/haynaku.htm.

Recipient of the Philippines' National Book Award for Poetry, **EILEEN TABIOS** has edited or co-edited five books of poetry, fiction and essays released in the United States.

Her poetry and editing projects have received numerous awards including the PEN/Oakland-Josephine Miles National Literary Award, The Potrero Nuevo Fund Prize, the Gustavus Meyers Outstanding Book Award in the Advancement of Human Rights, *Foreword Magazine's* Anthology of the Year Award, *Poet Magazine's* Iva Mary Williams Poetry Award, Judds Hill's Annual Poetry Prize and the Philippine American Writers & Artists' Catalagan Award; recognition from the Academy of American Poets, the Asian Pacific Association of Librarians and the PEN-Open Book Committee; as well as grants from the Witter Bynner Foundation, National Endowment of the Arts, the New York State Council on the Humanities, the California Council for the Humanities, and the New York City Downtown Cultural Council.

She edits the journal GALATEA RESURRECTS (A Poetry Engagement) (http://galatearesurrects.blogspot.com), performs the poetics blog "The Blind Chatelaine's Poker Poetics" (http://angelicpoker.blogspot.com) while all the time steering Meritage Press (www.meritagepress.com).

Ms Tabios is the Poet Laureate for Dutch Henry Winery in St. Helena, CA where, as a budding vintner, she is arduously and long-sufferingly researching the poetry of wine.